HEWLETT-WOODMERE PUBLIC LIBRARY
HEWLETT, NEW YORK

D1450699

577.54
N

Ecosystems Research Journal

Atacama Desert Research Journal

Sonya Newland

CRABTREE
PUBLISHING COMPANY
WWW.CRABTREEBOOKS.COM

CRABTREE
PUBLISHING COMPANY
WWW.CRABTREEBOOKS.COM

Author: Heather Hudak

Editors: Sonya Newland, Kathy Middleton

Design: Clare Nicholas

Cover design: Abigail Smith

Illustrator: Ron Dixon

Proofreader: Wendy Scavuzzo

Production coordinator and prepress technician: Tammy McGarr

Print coordinator: Katherine Berti

Produced for Crabtree Publishing Company by White-Thomson Publishing

Photo Credits:

Cover: All images from Shutterstock

Interior: Alamy: p. 7 James Brunker, p. 9r Ricardo Ribas, p. 10t James Brunker, p. 12t Danita Delimont, p. 15t Michele Burgess; iStock: pp. 4–5 filipefrazao, p. 12b alfnqn, p. 13t JeremyRichards, p. 13b 1001nights, p. 16 denisk0, p. 19t DarthArt, p. 19b miralex, p. 20t sara_winter, p. 20b agustavop, p. 21t Anne_Batzelona, p. 26t Wildnerpix, p. 29 1001nights; Getty Images: p. 22r Oliver Strewe, p. 23b Martin Bernetti; NASA: p. 21b CampoAlto/V. Robles; Shutterstock: p. 4 Nicholas Tinelli, p. 5 Ianaid12, pp. 6–7 Ivan F. Barreto, p. 8 JeremyRichards, pp. 8–9 lucas nishimoto, p. 9l Alice Nerr, p. 10b Bildagentur Zoonar GmbH, p. 11b Mariusz Potocki, p. 14 Anastasia Zenina-Lembrik, pp. 14–15 mmtsales, p. 15b Steve Allen, pp. 16–17 reisegraf.ch, p. 17 reisegraf.ch, p. 18 Natursports, p. 22l Marzolino, p. 23t Klopping, p. 24 Matt Amery, pp. 24–25 Elisa Locci, p. 25t reisegraf.ch, p. 25b, tocak, p. 27t Carlos D Pavletic, p. 27b Maurizio Bio, pp. 28–29; Wikimedia: p. 11t Hans Peter Möller, Jaime E. Jiménez, p.26b.

Library and Archives Canada Cataloguing in Publication

Newland, Sonya, author
    Atacama Desert research journal / Sonya Newland.

(Ecosystems research journal)
Includes index.
Issued in print and electronic formats.
ISBN 978-0-7787-4670-6 (hardcover).--
ISBN 978-0-7787-4683-6 (softcover).--
ISBN 978-1-4271-2067-0 (HTML)

    1. Atacama Desert (Chile)--Juvenile literature.
2. Biotic communities--Chile--Atacama Desert--Juvenile literature.
3. Desert ecology--Chile--Atacama Desert--Juvenile literature.
4. Ecology--Chile--Atacama Desert--Juvenile literature. I. Title.

QH119.N49 2018   j577.540983'14   C2017-907627-2
                            C2017-907628-0

Library of Congress Cataloging-in-Publication Data

CIP Available at the Library of Congress

Crabtree Publishing Company
www.crabtreebooks.com   1-800-387-7650

Printed in the U.S.A./022018/CG20171220

Copyright © **2018 CRABTREE PUBLISHING COMPANY**. All rights reserved. No part of this publication may be reproduced, stored in a retrieval system or be transmitted in any form or by any means, electronic, mechanical, photocopying, recording, or otherwise, without the prior written permission of Crabtree Publishing Company.

Published in Canada
Crabtree Publishing
616 Welland Ave.
St. Catharines, Ontario
L2M 5V6

Published in the United States
Crabtree Publishing
PMB 59051
350 Fifth Avenue, 59th Floor
New York, New York 10118

Published in the United Kingdom
Crabtree Publishing
Maritime House
Basin Road North, Hove
BN41 1WR

Published in Australia
Crabtree Publishing
3 Charles Street
Coburg North
VIC, 3058

3 1327 00651 2354

Contents

Mission to the Atacama Desert   4

Field Journal Day 1: Arica and the Azapa Valley   6

Field Journal Day 2: Pan-American Highway to Iquique   8

Field Journal Day 3: Pampa del Tamarugal National Reserve   10

Field Journal Day 4: Calama Oasis   12

Field Journal Day 5: Los Flamencos National Reserve   14

Field Journal Day 6: Chuquicamata Mine   16

Field Journal Day 7: San Pedro de Atacama and El Tatio   18

Field Journal Day 8: Death Valley and the Valley of the Moon   20

Field Journal Day 9: Lomas Near Paposo   22

Field Journal Day 10: Pan de Azúcar National Park   24

Field Journal Day 11: Copiapó   26

Final Report   28

Your Turn   30

Learning More   31

Glossary & Index   32

Mission to the Atacama Desert

I've just received an exciting email from the Global Desert Research Group! As an eremologist—a scientist who studies deserts—they want me to join a research trip to the Atacama Desert. The Atacama is a cool, **arid** desert that stretches about 600 miles (966 kilometers) along the coast of Chile in South America. We'll be investigating issues that are affecting the Atacama, and the plants, animals, and people that live there. I know that **climate change**, tourism, pollution, and **deforestation** are all having an impact on the desert. I hope I can help with some of the problems this amazing **ecosystem** faces.

↑ Many plants in the Atacama Desert cannot be found anywhere else in the world. This cactus, called Copiapoa cinerascens, is endangered.

Mountains and volcanoes lie on the border of the Atacama Desert. ↑

The Atacama is not like many other deserts. To begin with, it can get chilly there even during the day. The higher you go, the colder the air becomes—and the Atacama is high up! It lies on a **plateau** between two mountain ranges, the Andes and the Chilean Coast Range. In fact, the Atacama is the highest desert in the world. When you think of deserts, you probably think of sand. The Atacama is partly sandy, but a lot of it is stony. There are also salt lakes, canyons, and valleys. I'm told the red, rocky part of the desert looks like another world.

The Atacama Desert covers 40,540 square miles (105,000 square km).

I'm looking forward to seeing animals such as the llama–like guanaco on my trip.

Field Journal: Day 1

Arica and the Azapa Valley

Our journey begins in Arica. This city in northern Chile lies on the edge of the Atacama Desert. It is known as the driest place on Earth where people live. Arica gets less than 1/16 of an inch (1.5 millimeters) of rain in an entire year. That's actually more than in other parts of the Atacama! In some places, no rainfall has ever been recorded. Most fresh water comes from rivers that start high up in the mountains and flow down through the desert.

More than 1 million people live in the Atacama Desert, mostly along the coast.

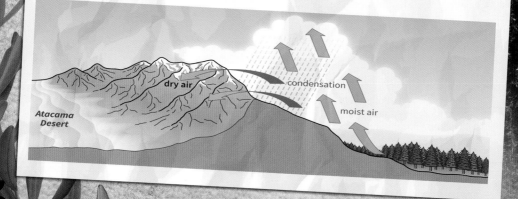

When mountains block moist air from reaching the other side of the mountains, rain falls only on one side. This is called a rain shadow. The Atacama is very dry because it lies in a double rain-shadow area, between two mountain ranges.

dry air

condensation

moist air

Atacama Desert

We travel by bus into the nearby Azapa Valley. There is good farmland here for growing fruits and vegetables. Water comes from springs. Canals were also built to bring more water from the Andes. This has allowed the city to spread into the valley. As we traveled farther in, I was amazed at how green the landscape was. I was hoping to spot a Chilean woodstar. The Azapa Valley is one of the few places where this critically endangered bird can still be found. The plants that the woodstar feeds on have died out nearly everywhere else. Sadly, I had no luck.

Rivers in the Atacama Desert

Loa	273 miles (440 kilometers)
Copiapó	101 miles (162 kilometers)
Del Carmen	90 miles (145 kilometers)
Huasco	55 miles (88 kilometers)
Salado	50 miles (80 kilometers)

The Azapa Valley is famous for its olives. ↘

Field Journal: Day 2

Pan-American Highway to Iquique

We set off down the **Pan-American Highway**. There were few signs of life. It seemed incredible that anything could survive in this arid environment. But when we arrived in Iquique it was a different story. The city was buzzing with life. Where there are lots of people, there are often threats to fragile ecosystems. As the population here has increased, the city has spread. This has resulted in habitat loss for plants and animals. More and more land is also being taken over for livestock to graze on.

Sightings

I spotted a southern viscacha resting on a rock. They look like rabbits with long tails, and they come out in the day to bask in the desert sunshine.

← Southern viscacha

Iquique is expanding into the surrounding desert. ↑

It's not all bad news, though. We find a place not far from the city, where a special plant thrives. *Tillandsia landbeckii* is a type of plant called an aerophyte. Aerophytes can **adapt** to survive in very harsh environments. Some get the **nutrients** they need by growing on other plants. *Tillandsia landbeckii* has adapted in a different way. It gets the moisture it needs from the air, not from the ground through its roots. This means it can grow in the dry desert soil.

Near Iquique is a 20,000-year-old sand dune known as Cerro Dragon. It was made a protected area in 2005 to preserve the habitat. I was disappointed to see that people still dump their trash on the dune.

Tillandsia landbeckii

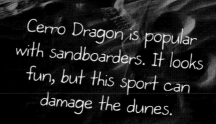

Cerro Dragon is popular with sandboarders. It looks fun, but this sport can damage the dunes.

Pampa del Tamarugal National Reserve

One of our trip's main goals is to observe conservation efforts at the Pampa del Tamarugal National Reserve. We headed there today to see the forests of tamarugo trees. It was certainly strange to see so many trees in a desert! Tamarugo trees can grow here because they have deep roots that find underground water. We joined the workers in the forest. They explained why the trees were under threat. Nearby towns and farms were using all the underground water. The tamarugos were also being cut down. Their wood was used to help build mines.

Tamarugo trees absorb water through their leaves as well as their roots.

The Atacama is famous for its **petroglyphs**. These carvings were made on the rock walls by people traveling through the area more than 1,000 years ago. There are more than 350 petroglyphs in the Tamarugal National Reserve.

To avoid damaging this important archaeological site, we do not touch the petroglyphs.

Tamarugo
↖ fruit

The tamarugo forests are here today because of a successful conservation project. New trees were planted and laws were introduced to protect the area. Visitors to the reserve are now taught about the trees and wildlife. This is an important area for animals and birds such as the rare tamarugo conebill. But there are new threats to the forest. People still cut down the trees illegally. Too many animals are grazed on the land. This damages the soil. People dig wells and drain the underground water. Today, 25 percent of the trees here are dead or dying.

A chilla fox stopped and stared
↖ as we explored the forest.

natstat STATUS REPORT ST456/part B

Name:

Tamarugo conebill
(Conirostrum tamarugense)

Threats:

Habitat loss

Description:

The tamarugo conebill is named after the tamarugo tree. It has bright red feathers on its face, neck, and under its tail. The conebill feeds on insects, such as caterpillars, that are attracted to the trees. It only breeds in northern Chile.

Numbers:

35,000

Status:

Least concern

Field Journal: Day 4

Calama Oasis

We've moved away from the coast and are spending a few days in Calama, in the heart of the Atacama. Calama is a city built around an oasis, which is a place in the desert where water is found. Land surrounding it is too dry to grow crops, but an oasis provides enough water for **irrigation**. We saw farmers tending fields of alfalfa and potatoes. Settlements often grow up around desert oases. The oasis at Calama has grown to become a city of 150,000 people. It has hotels, restaurants, an airport, and even an amusement park.

Local people refer to Calama as "the city of sun and copper" because of the copper mining industry in the area. $\longrightarrow$

Every 5 to 7 years, a weather effect called El Niño causes more rain than usual in the Atacama. When this happens, parts of the desert come alive with flowers. $\longrightarrow$

The Loa River is the longest river in Chile. It flows through Calama. Mining is an important industry here. Water from the Loa is used to generate **hydroelectric power** for the mines nearby. But the mines are also polluting the river that powers them. Harmful waste is dumped into the Loa. This can be dangerous, because the river also provides drinking water for the people who live around the oases. Treatment systems can clean the water, but they are expensive. The Chilean National Environmental Commission is working to improve water treatment facilities across the Atacama Desert.

The Loa River starts in the Andes mountains and flows all the way to the Pacific Ocean.

natstat STATUS REPORT ST456/part B

Name: Vicuña (Vicugna vicugna)

Threats: Poaching and habitat loss

Description:
The shy, grass-eating vicuña is related to the llama. It can grow to about 5 feet (1.5 meters) in length and stands about 3 feet (0.9 meters) high. Its long brown coat produces a very fine wool. This has made it a target for **poachers**. Conservation programs over the past 50 years have been very successful, though, and the vicuña is no longer under threat.

Numbers: 350,000

Status: Nearly extinct by the 1970s; now least concern

Attach photograph here

Field Journal: Day 5

Los Flamencos National Reserve

There are several oases in this part of the Atacama. They have been home to desert people for thousands of years. This gives us the perfect opportunity to focus our research on people who live in the desert. The **Indigenous** Atacameños were once **nomads**. They hunted llamas and followed the herds across the desert. Over time, their ways of life changed. They settled around the oases. They learned to manage the water so they could grow maize, or corn. We spoke to a group of Atacameños. They told us how their traditional ways of life were being threatened. A few years ago, mining was the biggest problem. Mining companies took over the land and polluted the water. Now, tourism poses an additional threat.

Los Flamencos National Reserve

Sightings

We saw lots of Andean flamingos. The nature reserve is named for them. They feed on a type of water plant called algae in the salt lakes.

Andean flamingo

Los Flamencos National Reserve was established in 1990. The government and the Atacameños care for this protected area together. In some ways, this has helped the Indigenous people. Many Atacameños earn a living by working in the park. But tourism is still a problem. More than 300,000 visitors a year come to Los Flamencos. Hotels have been built for them, which uses up land. The tourists use a lot of the limited fresh water. The Atacameños now have to use water that has flowed through salty land. This is not good for drinking. They also feel that the tourists do not want to know about the Atacameños' history and culture. If visitors do not understand this, they will not help preserve their traditional lifestyle.

A sign teaches visitors about the history of the Atacameños.

Salt flats are large areas of desert covered with salt. They are created when a salt lake dries up quickly. Salt is left on the surface.

Field Journal: Day 6

Chuquicamata Mine

Mining has clearly had the biggest impact on the ecosystem in the Atacama. Today, we set off for the Chuquicamata copper mine to find out more. As we approached the mine, I saw empty houses and stores. The mine workers and their families once lived here. Pollution from the mining process forced them to move away. Dangerous gases polluted the air. A layer of black soot covered the ground for miles. There are now laws that make mining companies responsible for checking the air quality. Pollution has been reduced in many places—even here—but it is still not safe for people to live here.

Sightings

I spotted a Darwin's leaf-eared mouse disappearing into the cracks in some rocks a short distance from the mine.

Darwin's leaf-eared mouse

Chuquicamata is the largest open-pit mine (one that is not underground) in the world.

The town may be gone but the mine is still operating. Workers travel in from Calama each day. Roads are needed to transport people and materials to and from the mines. Road-building has disturbed the soil. This has caused habitat loss and damaged the desert ecosystem. But the Atacama is rich in copper and **minerals**. There are also gold and silver mines. The mining industry brings in a lot of money to the Atacama region. It is not always easy to have both a healthy environment and a healthy **economy**.

Traffic at the Chuquicamata mine

Chuquicamata Facts

Depth: 2,790 feet (850 meters)

Height: 9,350 feet (2,850 meters) above sea level

Area: 5 square miles (13 square kilometers)

Annual copper production: 650,000 tons (589,670 metric tons)

Total lifetime copper production: 29 million tons (26 million metic tons)

Field Journal: Day 7

San Pedro de Atacama and El Tatio

We arrived in San Pedro yesterday. This is the main town within the Atacama. It used to be a mining center. Now it is a popular tourist resort. San Pedro is close to some of the Atacama's most stunning landscapes. The streets here are packed with people. Most of them are here to take tours into the surrounding desert. The vehicles that travel to, from, and around these sites damage the soil. Some tourist companies now offer hiking tours, which are less harmful to the environment. But I still saw many cars and buses heading out of town.

The church in San Pedro de Atacama →

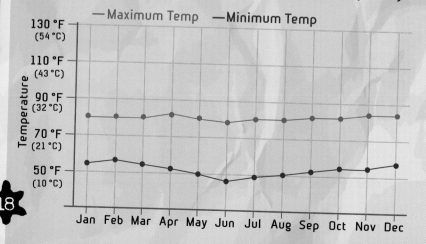

Average Daytime Temperatures in San Pedro de Atacama
Although it is very dry, the Atacama is not a hot desert. Temperatures range from 32 °F (0 °C) to 77 °F (25 °C).

— Maximum Temp — Minimum Temp

Temperature

130 °F (54 °C)
110 °F (43 °C)
90 °F (32 °C)
70 °F (21 °C)
50 °F (10 °C)

Jan Feb Mar Apr May Jun Jul Aug Sep Oct Nov Dec

We set out before dawn this morning to reach El Tatio. One of the main tourist attractions in the Atacama, this area has about 80 **geysers**. People come here to bathe in these hot pools. A few years ago, work began on a project to harness the **geothermal power** of the geysers to create electricity. The project was canceled but the idea hasn't gone away. Mining companies want to explore this area, too. They think there may be other useful resources beneath the ground, not just water. Many people are against these projects. They argue that they would pollute and change the landscape forever.

Buses carry thousands of tourists around the desert every year.

El Tatio geysers

The geysers are at their most impressive early in the morning. This is because the contrast between the very cold air and the boiling water makes the column of water shoot higher. The geysers can reach more than 3 feet (1 meter) into the air.

19

Field Journal: Day 8

Death Valley and the Valley of the Moon

Wow—two amazing valleys in one day! The Valle de la Muerte (Death Valley) is a short hike from San Pedro. From a viewpoint on a high rock, we could see the volcanoes that border the Atacama. One of these, Ojos del Salado, is the highest active volcano in the world. The Atacama lies in the Ring of Fire. This is land that rings the Pacific Ocean where a lot of earthquakes and eruptions take place. Many of the volcanoes here have not erupted in more than 1,000 years, but some still do. Lascar volcano had a small eruption in 2015, and a bigger eruption in 1993. Lava flows eroded the rock around the volcano and covered the land nearby in ash. The ash also caused air and water pollution that took months to clear.

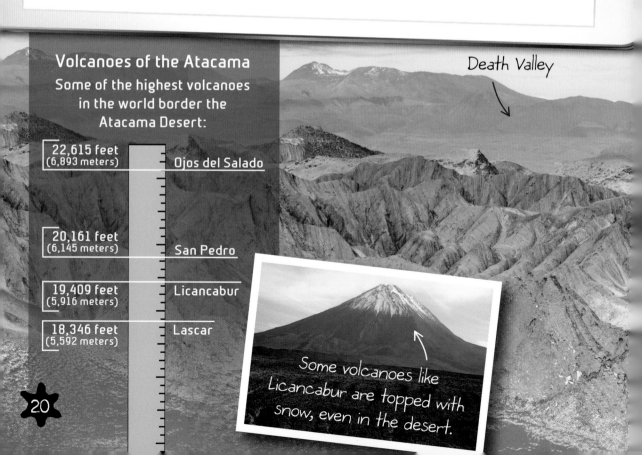

Volcanoes of the Atacama

Some of the highest volcanoes in the world border the Atacama Desert:

22,615 feet (6,893 meters)	Ojos del Salado
20,161 feet (6,145 meters)	San Pedro
19,409 feet (5,916 meters)	Licancabur
18,346 feet (5,592 meters)	Lascar

Death Valley

Some volcanoes like Licancabur are topped with snow, even in the desert.

The rocks and dunes in the Valley of the Moon are shaped by the wind. Some dunes are changing constantly. ↘

A NASA rover test drilling in the Atacama.

The landscape here is so unusual that I feel like I've stepped into another world. In fact, space agencies test out the vehicles they use on Mars in this part of the desert! No plants or animals live here.

We moved from a valley shaped by volcanoes to one shaped by wind. The Valley of the Moon is in the Salt mountain range. The landscape here is a mix of high sand dunes, dramatic rock formations, and huge salt flats. The valley is part of the Los Flamencos National Reserve. Chile's Corporación Nacional Forestal (CONAF), or National Forest Corporation, shares responsibility for the valley with the Indigenous Association of the Moon Valley. The Indigenous group is made up of several local communities. They work together to make sure that tourists do not harm the environment. Staff patrol the area. They make sure that no one wanders off the marked paths.

Field Journal: Day 9

Lomas Near Paposo

Heading back down toward the Pacific coast, we stop at Paposo. This is a tiny settlement, but Paposo is a special place in the Atacama. In most parts of the desert, only a few cactuses and grasses can survive. Near Paposo, an amazing variety of plants and flowers flourish. They grow in what is known as a loma, or fog oasis. Fog from the Pacific Ocean builds up here. The moisture in the fog allows plants to thrive. There are lomas in other parts of the Atacama, but the lomas near Paposo have more plant species than any other. These provide food and shelter for animals, birds, and insects.

About 1,000 people live in Paposo. Many of them fish for a living.

Sightings

I spotted a giant hummingbird feeding on the nectar of the flowers in the blooming lomas.

Giant hummingbird

The lomas are vital to the survival of many plants. But more than 35 percent of the species here are under threat due to deforestation and overgrazing by farm animals. The government of Chile has made the lomas at Paposo a protected zone. Researchers like us come here to learn about desert plants. We are particularly interested in the plants that only grow in the Atacama, such as the flowering shrubs *Euphorbia lactiflua* and *Oxalis gigantea*. Tourists are also encouraged to visit the lomas. It is important to teach people how vital the lomas are. That way, they will understand why the lomas should be protected. This is called ecotourism. Despite efforts, local people still graze their goats here. This can damage the soil and the plants.

Species of the flowering plant ← Nolana grow in the lomas.

Local people use the fog as a water source. They hang up plastic sheets with buckets underneath. The fog **condenses** on the plastic and the water runs into the buckets. It is used for watering crops in drier parts of the desert.

Organizations use a similar system to get water from fog. They hang nets with troughs ↗ beneath them.

Field Journal: Day 10

Pan de Azúcar National Park

We wanted to continue our research on plants in the Atacama. This led us to the Pan de Azúcar National Park. About 27 different species of cactuses grow here. Our first stop was CONAF's information center. CONAF is a government agency. It works on programs to protect Chile's forests. It also protects other ecosystems, including parts of the Atacama Desert. CONAF has a garden called a cactarium near the park. All the different cactuses are on display there. Most of them are types of Copiapoa. This species is often found in dry coastal areas like this part of the Atacama.

Pan de Azúcar National Park was established in 1986.

Isla Pan de Azúcar

We took a boat to Isla Pan de Azúcar. This island lies off the coast of the national park. People are not allowed on the island but from the boat, I could see Humboldt penguins. These birds breed on the island.

Our hosts from CONAF took us out into the park. They explained how cactuses survive in such a dry desert. Their roots spread out to absorb as much water as possible. They store water inside their prickly stems. This keeps them alive through long, dry periods. Amazingly, their spines stop air from flowing too close to the plant's stem, protecting the cactus from drying out. Cactuses are important in the desert ecosystem. They are a vital source of food and water for birds, animals, and insects. Our guides say that there are plans to expand the park farther north. That way, they can protect more of these precious plants.

Flowers on some cactuses such as this Copiapoa provide nectar for birds such as hummingbirds.

natstat STATUS REPORT ST456/part B

Name: Humboldt penguin
(Spheniscus humboldti)

Description:

These are medium-sized penguins. They have black backs and tails. They also have a black band running down their chest to their feet. Humboldt penguins mate for life. They lay one or two eggs in sand burrows or in crevices in rocks and cliffs. Both male and female penguins take care of the chicks.

Threats:
Overfishing, which reduces their food source; climate change

Numbers: 3,300–12,000

Status: Vulnerable

Attach photograph here

Copiapó

We've reached our final destination. As we drove into the town of Copiapó, I saw a culpeo fox at the side of the road. It was feasting on a rabbit. We haven't seen many animals on our journey. The desert is too dry even for many insects to survive, but culpeo foxes can be found all over the Atacama. They prey on smaller animals. They are important because they help keep down the numbers of rabbits. European rabbits are an **introduced species** in the desert. Settlers bred them for food and to sell their fur. The rabbits are considered pests, and they eat the precious desert plants. But some people think the culpeo foxes are also pests. They have been known to attack livestock.

Culpeo fox →

natstat STATUS REPORT ST456/part B

Name: Short-tailed chinchilla (*Chinchilla chinchilla*)	**Threats:** Illegal hunting; habitat loss from mining
	Numbers: Unknown
Description: Short-tailed chinchillas are large rodents. They can grow up to 20 inches (50 centimeters) long. They live in groups and make their homes in burrows under rocks. They have very soft gray fur, which keeps them warm in the cold desert nights. This fur has made them attractive to hunters.	**Status:** Critically endangered in Chile

Attach photograph here →

26

Wind turbines on the road from Caldera
↓

The entrance to an old silver mine near Copiapó
↓

We have come to Copiapó to find out about renewable energy projects. Renewable energy is power created by a source that will not run out, such as wind and sunshine. Deserts are good places to build wind and solar farms. Both types of energy are being produced in this part of the Atacama. The government of Chile has set a renewable energy target. It wants the country to get 20 percent of its energy from renewable resources by 2020 instead of from oil and gas. The roads from the coast to Copiapó are lined with wind turbines. A solar farm was opened in 2014. It now provides more than 125,000 households in Chile with energy. It's great to see the desert's resources being used without damaging the area.

In 2010, 33 miners were trapped after a cave-in at the San José mine near Copiapó. They were underground for 69 days before they were rescued. Workers above ground drilled a hole and sent down food and water.

Final Report

THE GLOBAL DESERT RESEARCH GROUP

OBSERVATIONS

The Atacama Desert is one of the harshest environments in the world. Only the toughest plants and animals live there. They have adapted to survive on limited resources. Despite the dry landscape, there are areas where life thrives. The fog oases create a moisture-rich environment for plants to grow. Rivers and springs created oases. People settled there and used the water to grow crops. Out in the desert near San Pedro de Atacama are vast salt flats and lakes. The lakes provide water for flamingos, vicuñas, and other species. But these important areas in the desert may be at risk.

Even in the desert, plants and animals find water to help them survive.

28

FUTURE CONCERNS

Chile is becoming an increasingly popular tourist destination. This is good for the economy, but not all tourists respect the fragile desert ecosystem. They may cause damage that can never be fixed. Local people are also harming the environment. They graze livestock and dig wells on protected land. Big mining companies are still building roads that cut through precious desert land. Care must also be taken when building new solar farms. Soil damage could drive away animals and kill plants. Proper management of water resources in the desert is probably the most urgent concern. Without water, no plants, animals, or people would be able to live here.

CONSERVATION PROJECTS

CONAF carries out research all over Chile. It also manages the national parks within the Atacama Desert. Tree-planting programs in these areas help preserve the soil, plants, and animal habitats. I've noticed that many protected areas focus a lot on education. They aim to teach visitors how important the ecosystem is. Some plants native to the Atacama have already been lost forever. To stop this from happening, scientists from the Agricultural Research Institute in Chile are collecting seeds. These will be put in the Millennium Seed Bank. This special place in the United Kingdom stores seeds of many plants to make sure they will never die out. New laws are making mining companies face their responsibilities to reduce air and water pollution. All these efforts are important. They will help keep the future of this incredible environment safe.

Vicuña

Your Turn

✱ Choose one of the animals or birds mentioned in this book, or another animal that lives in the Atacama Desert. Find out more about it. You could choose a llama or alpaca, or one of the foxes—culpeo or chilla. Perhaps you might like to find out more about the Andean flamingo. Write your own "Status Report" about your chosen animal. In the description, include information about how it has adapted to survive in the desert. Name some of the threats it faces and find out whether it is endangered.

✱ Look back at the information about the Indigenous Atacameños people on pages 14–15. Imagine you go to visit one of their settlements in the Atacama Desert. Write a journal entry describing what you learn about their history and culture. What do they tell you about the problems they face? What do you think would help them?

✱ Tourism is important for the economy of the Atacama region. But lots of tourists can harm the environment. Imagine you are going to set up a sustainable tour company in San Pedro de Atacama. Find out about the different things there are to do in the area. Then think how you could make tours to these places environmentally friendly. Create an itinerary, or schedule.

Learning More

BOOKS

The Atacama Desert (Deserts Around the World) by Lynn Peppas (Crabtree Publishing Company, 2012)

Deserts Inside Out by Marina Cohen (Crabtree Publishing Company, 2015)

Desert Survival Guide by Ruth Owen (Crabtree Publishing Company, 2010)

WEBSITES

www.dogonews.com/2010/7/19/atacama-desert-the-worlds-driest-desert
Find out about the world's driest desert in this article from DOGOnews.

http://pubs.usgs.gov/gip/deserts/contents/
This website gives an overview of deserts and their resources.

http://ngm.nationalgeographic.com/ngm/0308/feature3/
Find out how people survive in the driest place on Earth in this article from National Geographic.

www.factmonster.com/world/world-geography/principal-deserts-world
Learn all about the world's deserts, including the Atacama.

Glossary & Index

adapt to change over time to become better suited to an ecosystem

arid very dry

climate change a change in the normal weather in an area over time, caused by pollution and other human actions

condenses turns from liquid to gas or vapor

deforestation the cutting down of trees to make way for grazing land and expanding cities

economy the money that goes into and out of a particular area

ecosystem a community of plants, animals, and their environment

geothermal power natural energy that comes from heat in Earth

geysers naturally occurring hot springs that sometimes shoot jets of water in the air

hydroelectric power electricity generated by the power of moving water

Indigenous native to an area

introduced species a plant or animal that does not live or grow naturally in an ecosystem and which can damage it

irrigation supplying water to land or crops to help things grow

minerals solid substances that occur naturally in the ground

nomads people who move around rather than settling in one place

nutrients substances that living things need to survive and grow

Pan-American Highway a road that stretches 18,640 miles (30,000 kilometers) from Alaska in North America to Panama in South America

petroglyphs pictures of people, animals, and shapes carved into natural landscapes

plateau an area of high, flat land

poachers people who hunt animals illegally

Andean flamingos 14, 28
Arica 5, 6, 7
Atacameños 14, 15
Azapa Valley 6, 7

cactuses 4, 22, 24, 25
Calama 5, 12, 13, 17
Chilean woodstar 7
chilla fox 11
Chuquicamata 5, 16, 17
climate change 4, 25
CONAF 21, 24, 25, 29
Chilean National Environmental Commission 13
conservation projects 10, 11, 13, 24, 29
Copiapó 5, 26, 27
culpeo fox 26

Darwin's leaf-eared mouse 16
Death Valley 5, 20
deforestation 4, 11, 23

El Niño 12
El Tatio geysers 5, 19

farming 7, 10, 12

geothermal power 19
giant hummingbird 22

habitat loss 8, 11, 17, 26
Humboldt penguins 24, 25
hydroelectric power 13

Indigenous Association of the Moon Valley 21
introduced species 26
Iquique 5, 8, 9
irrigation 12
Isla Pan de Azúcar 24

laws 11, 16, 29
livestock grazing 8, 23, 26, 29
Loa River 7, 13
lomas 22, 23, 28
Los Flamencos 14, 15, 21

mining 12, 13, 14, 16, 17, 18, 19, 26, 27, 29
mountains 4, 5, 6, 7, 13, 21

oases 12, 13, 14, 28
Ojos del Salado 20

Pampa del Tamarugal 10
Pan de Azúcar 24, 25
Pan-American Highway 5, 8
Paposo 5, 22, 23
petroglyphs 10
poaching 13
pollution 4, 13, 14, 16, 19, 20, 29

rainfall 6, 12
rain shadow effect 6
renewable energy 27
rivers 6, 7, 13, 28

salt flats 15, 21, 28
salt lakes 5, 28

San Pedro de Atacama 5, 18, 19, 20, 28
short-tailed chinchilla 26
southern visacha 8

tamarugo conebill 11
Tillandsia landbeckii 9
tourism 4, 14, 15, 18, 19, 21, 23, 29

Valley of the Moon 5, 20, 21
vicuñas 13, 28, 29
volcanoes 4, 20, 21

water 6, 7, 10, 11, 12, 13, 14, 15, 19, 23, 25, 28, 29